Johannes Brahms

Concerto for Violin and Orchestra in D major / D-Dur

Op. 77

Edited by / Herausgegeben von
Richard Clarke

EULENBURG

EAS 126
ISBN 978-3-7957-6526-2
ISMN M-2002-2349-1

Edition based on Eulenburg Study Score ETP 716

Ernst Eulenburg Ltd
48 Great Marlborough Street
London W1F 7BB

Contents / Inhalt

Preface

Composed: 1874, Vienna; 1877–78, Pörtschach
First performance: 1 January 1879 in Leipzig with Joseph Joachim as soloist and Johannes Brahms as conductor
Original publisher: Simrock, Berlin, 1879
Instrumentation: 2 Flutes, 2 Oboes, 2 Clarinets, 2 Bassoons – 4 Horns, 2 Trumpets – Timpani – Strings
Duration: ca. 40 minutes

The genesis of Brahms's Violin Concerto in D major Op. 77 is in many ways inseparable from the name of its dedicatee, Joseph Joachim (1831–1907). Brahms first heard Joachim in March 1848, when the violinist, not yet 17 years old but destined to become arguably the most celebrated violin virtuoso of the second half of the 19th century, had played the Beethoven concerto. 'Time and again', the composer later wrote to Joachim, 'the [Beethoven] concerto reminds me of our first encounter, of which you, of course, know nothing. You played it in Hamburg, [...] and I was undoubtedly your most enthusiastic listener'. But it was not until the end of May 1853 that the two men first met in Hannover, where Joachim was principal violinist to the house of Hannover. Their mutual sympathy and profound respect for each other as musicians soon matured into a lasting friendship, in the course of which Joachim introduced Brahms to numerous violin concertos, including Giovanni Battista Viotti's Violin Concerto No. 22 in A minor, a work that Brahms particularly admired. And Brahms in turn appears to have advised Joachim when he came to write his own Violin Concerto 'in the Hungarian style'. It was a friendship, finally, in which – to quote the composer's biographer, Max Kalbeck – Brahms 'very soon conceived the idea of writing a really beautiful work for the royal instrument of his beloved Jussuf [Joseph], a work that would be both great and demanding and entirely worthy of that instrument'.

In the event it was not until the summer of 1878, when Brahms was staying at Pörtschach on the Wörthersee, that this idea was finally realised. Brahms had spent the previous summer, too, in this delightful corner of rural Carinthia, working on his Second Symphony, and on that occasion he had described the region in a letter to his friend Eduard Hanslick as 'virginal territory, melodies fly through the air here and you must be careful not to tread on them'. Twelve years later he recalled his time in Pörtschach: 'Beautiful summer days come to mind and, involuntarily, so too do many of the works that I took with me on my walks – the D major Symphony, the Violin Concerto, the G major Sonata, the Rhapsodies and the like. And "is the old man still alive"? I mean the old priest, that frivolous old joker. His laughter could be heard (literally) across the lake, his extremely bad jokes even as far away as Vienna.' The absence of relevant sources makes it impossible for us to know if Brahms wrote down his Violin Concerto in the summer of 1878 on the basis of existing sketches and drafts or whether he in fact composed it in its entirety in Pörtschach in 1878. By the same token, we can only speculate on the reasons why Brahms waited until the summer of 1878 to write such a work: after all, he had first met Joachim a quarter of a century earlier. Perhaps it was the worldwide success of his Second Symphony, which had received its first performance in Vienna on 30 December 1877 and which, confirming its composer's now incontrovertible reputation, helped to overcome the lacerating self-doubts characteristic of his career until now, that gave him the confidence to return to the concerto as a genre after his successful engagement with the symphony. After all, the first performance of his Piano Concerto No. 1 in D minor Op. 15 in Hannover on 22 January 1859 had been the greatest artistic débâcle of his life. It is ultimately also impossible to know whether it was not only his friendship with Joachim that persuaded him to choose the violin as a solo instrument but also – as Kalbeck suggests – the playing of the Spanish virtuoso Pablo de Sarasate, whom Brahms heard in Baden-Baden in the autumn of 1877 rehearsing Max Bruch's Violin Concerto No. 2 in D minor Op. 44.

By contrast, the final phase in the concerto's genesis is rather more fully documented, and here we know that Joachim played an active role. On 22 August 1878 Brahms sent him a parcel containing the solo part of the opening movement and a letter couched in the ironic and witty language that the composer – a pianist, rather than a violinist by training – often adopted in his correspondence: 'I'll be satisfied if you say the odd word and perhaps write your comments into it [i.e., into the violin part]: difficult, awkward, impossible, that sort of thing. The whole thing has four movements, I'm writing the beginning of the last one so that the awkward passages are forbidden me right away!' Joachim lost no time in responding to Brahms's request, writing his suggested changes into the solo part and spelling them out in greater detail at two subsequent meetings that he held with the composer, the first in Pörtschach at the end of August 1878, the second in Hamburg at the end of September 1878. No doubt he additionally demonstrated them on his violin. He also wrote the opening movement's solo cadenza.

There was no question in Brahms's mind that Joachim should give the first performance, and yet he seems to have been disconcerted by the haste with which the violinist insisted on bringing forward the date of that performance. As early as the middle of October 1878 Joachim was already writing to announce that he was thinking of playing it at the traditional New Year concert in Leipzig and therefore needed it in its entirety very soon, prompting Brahms to write back to say that he 'did not like to be rushed when writing and performing' his music, especially because in the present case he was now revising what had been planned as a four-movement work and turning it into a traditional three-movement concerto. Brahms must have been working on these revisions as late as November, for in a letter to Joachim we find him reporting that 'The middle movements have fallen in battle – needless to add, they were the best! But I'll have a poor Adagio [the second movement of the finished work] written for it.' It was the middle of December by the time that Joachim received the new solo part of what was now a three-movement work. Yet, in spite of the pressure of time, it was still not too late for the concerto to be premièred at the Leipzig New Year concert on 1 January 1879 with the Gewandhaus Orchestra under Brahms's direction. Joachim was the soloist.

'In sum', wrote Alfred Dörffel in the *Leipziger Nachrichten*, reporting on the initial reaction to the concerto, 'the first movement prevented its audience from noticing what was novel about the work, but the second movement left a very real impression; and the final movement gave rise to much cheering.' Both in Leipzig and at the work's first performance in Vienna on 14 January 1879, the critics agreed that this 'may be described as the most important concerto to have appeared since those of Beethoven and Mendelssohn'. It was above all the symphonic dimension of the work that contributed to this sense of importance. The solo instrument does not dominate, and the soloist's abilities are not privileged in any way. Rather, violin and orchestra merge in the sense of a higher musical unity. In spite of this, the writing for the solo violin is extremely virtuosic with its multiple stopping, rapid changes of position and passage-work. Yet none of these are an end in themselves. Instead, they are fully integrated into a structure in which the themes are symphonically presented, reworked and developed with all the expressive variety of the musical language of the Pörtschach Brahms: the writing is by turns brooding, serenade-like, pastoral and what Hanslick termed 'garden music'. Passages of great seriousness appear alongside others that are playful and witty, most notably in the third movement, an *Allegro giocoso*. Like the Second Symphony that Brahms had written in Pörtschach the previous summer, the work as a whole is imbued with a sense of carefree amiability that in Simrock's words is 'full of sunshine'.

Klaus Döge
Translation: Stewart Spencer

Vorwort

Komponiert: 1874 in Wien, 1877/78 in Pörtschach
Uraufführung: 1. Januar 1879 in Leipzig mit Joseph Joachim als Solisten und Johannes Brahms als Dirigenten
Originalverlag: Simrock, Berlin, 1879
Orchesterbesetzung: 2 Flöten, 2 Oboen, 2 Klarinetten, 2 Fagotte – 4 Hörner, 2 Trompeten – Pauken – Streicher
Spieldauer: etwa 40 Minuten

Die Entstehung des Violinkonzerts D-Dur, op. 77 ist in mehrfacher Hinsicht eng mit dem Geiger Joseph Joachim (1831–1907), dem Brahms sein Konzert widmete, verbunden. Erstmals hatte Brahms im März 1848 diesen wohl berühmtesten Violinvirtuosen der zweiten Hälfte des 19. Jahrhunderts in einem Konzert erlebt, in dem das damals noch nicht ganz 17 Jahre alte Geigenwunder das Beethoven'sche Violinkonzert spielte. „Immer und immer", so schrieb der Komponist darüber später an Joachim, „erinnert mich das [Beethoven'sche] Konzert an unsere erste Bekanntschaft, von der Du freilich nichts weißt. Du spieltest es in Hamburg […], und ich war Dein begeistertster Zuhörer." Persönlich bekannt wurde Brahms mit Joachim Ende Mai 1853 in Hannover, wo der angesehene Geiger als königlicher Konzertmeister wirkte. Aus ihrer gegenseitigen Sympathie sowie aus ihrer gegenseitigen Hochschätzung als Künstler entwickelte sich bald eine tiefe Freundschaft, – eine Freundschaft, in der Joachim Johannes Brahms mit zahlreichen Violinkonzerten (darunter das von Brahms hochgeschätzte Violinkonzert a-Moll, Nr. 22, von Giovanni Battista Viotti) vertraut machte und Brahms dem Geiger bei der Komposition von dessen Ungarischen Konzert für Violine und Orchester anscheinend beratend zur Seite stand; und eine Freundschaft schließlich, in der – wie der Brahms-Biograph Max Kalbeck schreibt – „es schon früh ein Lieblingsgedanke des Komponisten war, der königlichen Geige seines geliebten Jussuf etwas recht Schönes zuzuwenden mit einem ihrer würdigen, großen und schweren Werke."

Verwirklicht hat Brahms diesen Gedanken allerdings erst im Sommer 1878 in Pörtschach am Wörthersee, in jener ländlich so anmutigen Gegend Kärntens, die er ein Jahr zuvor (in Zusammenhang mit der Komposition der 2. Sinfonie) seinem Freund Eduard Hanslick gegenüber mit dem Satz, „der Wörther See ist ein jungfräulicher Boden, da fliegen die Melodien, daß man [sich] hüten muß, keine zu treten", schilderte und an die er sich 12 Jahre später mit den Worten erinnerte: „Schöne Sommertage kommen mir in den Sinn und willkürlich Manches, mit dem ich dort spazieren ging, so die D-dur Symphonie, Violinkonzert und Sonate G-dur, Rhapsodien und derlei. Und lebt denn der alte Hauschild noch? Nämlich der alte, höchst lustige und frivole Pfaffe dort? Sein Lachen hörte man über den See (buchstäblich) und seine sehr schlimmen Witze bis Wien." Ob er im Sommer 1878 dabei auf der Grundlage von bereits zuvor notierten Skizzen und Entwürfen sein Violinkonzert niederschrieb oder ob er wirklich erst 1878 in Pörtschach das Werk als Ganzes neu komponierte, lässt sich fehlender Quellen wegen nicht sagen. Und auch hinsichtlich der Frage, warum Brahms erst im Sommer 1878 – immerhin 25 Jahre nach seinem ersten persönlichen Zusammentreffen mit Joseph Joachim – das geplante Violinkonzert vollendete, lassen sich nur Vermutungen anstellen: Möglicherweise hat der weltweite Erfolg (und damit Brahms' unumstößliche Anerkennung als Komponist) der 2. Sinfonie von ihrer Wiener Uraufführung am 30. Dezember 1877 an jene selbstzerfleischenden Skrupel, die Brahms' Künstlertum bis dahin immer wieder kennzeichneten, schaffenspsychologisch soweit gelockert, daß er jetzt – nach dem Erfolg mit der Gattung ‚Sinfonie' – sich kompositorisch erstmals wieder jener Gattung ‚Konzert' zuzuwenden getraute, mit der er bei der Uraufführung seines 1. Klavierkonzerts (d-Moll op. 15) am 22. Januar 1859 in Hannover sein größtes künstlerisches Debakel erleben musste. Ob dabei für die Wahl der Violine als Soloinstrument neben der Freundschaft zu Joachim wirklich auch das – wie Kalbeck annimmt – Spiel des spanischen Geigenvirtuosen Pablo de Sarasate, den Brahms im Herbst 1877 in Baden-Baden bei einer Probe des 2. Violinkonzerts (d-Moll, op. 44) von Max Bruch erlebte, „möglicherweise mit seinem faszinierendem Spiel, das gern in den höchsten Regionen des Griffbretts schwelgte, den entscheidenden Anstoß" gab, ist letztendlich nicht zu beantworten.

Besser dokumentiert dagegen ist die letzte Phase der Entstehung. Joseph Joachim wirkte in ihr aktiv mit. Am 22. August 1878 schickt Brahms ihm ein Päckchen, das die Solostimme des ersten Satzes des neuen Violinkonzerts sowie ein Schreiben enthielt, in dem der Komponist, der selbst Pianist und kein voll ausgebildeter Geigenspieler war, in seinem mitunter oft recht ironisch-witzigen Briefstil schrieb: „Ich bin zufrieden, wenn Du ein Wort sagst, und vielleicht einige [in die Stimme] hineinschreibst: schwer, unbequem, unmöglich usw. Die ganze Geschichte hat vier Sätze, vom letzten schreib ich den Anfang – damit mir gleich die ungeschickten Figuren verboten werden!" Joachim ist der Bitte unmittelbar nachgekommen und hat seine in der Solostimme niedergeschriebenen Änderungsvorschläge auf zwei Zusammentreffen zwischen Komponist und Violinvirtuosen – das erste Ende August 1878 in Pörtschach, das zweite Ende September 1878 in Hamburg – konkretisiert und wohl auch auf seiner Geige demonstriert. Darüber hinaus schrieb er für den ersten Satz die Solo-Kadenz.

Dass Joachim angesichts all dessen auch das Primat der Uraufführung zustand, war für Brahms keine Frage. Irgendwie aber scheint ihn die Eile befremdet zu haben, mit der Joachim diese erste Aufführung forcierte. Als der Violinvirtuose ihm bereits Mitte Oktober 1878 mitteilte, dass er an eine Uraufführung im Rahmen des traditionellen Leipziger Neujahrskonzerts denke und er daher bald das Konzert in toto brauche, ließ Brahms ihn wissen, dass er „nicht gern eilig beim Schreiben und beim Aufführen" sei, – und dies umso mehr, als er gerade das ursprünglich viersätzig geplante Werk zu einem traditionell dreisätzigen Konzert umarbeite. Noch im November muss den Komponisten diese Umarbeitung beschäftigt zu haben, denn in einem Brief an seinen geigespielenden Freund hieß es damals: „Die Mittelsätze sind gefallen – natürlich waren es die besten! Ein armes Adagio [= der endgültige 2. Satz des Violinkonzerts] aber lasse ich dazu schreiben..." Die neu angefertigte Solostimme des jetzt dreisätzigen Werks erhielt Joachim erst Mitte Dezember 1878, – trotz der drängenden Zeit aber nicht zu spät, um am 1. Januar 1879 das Violinkonzert im Leipziger Neujahrskonzert mit Joseph Joachim als Solist und dem Gewandhausorchester unter der Leitung von Johannes Brahms zur Uraufführung zu bringen.

„Der Erfolg war: der 1. Satz ließ das Neue in der Zuhörerschaft nicht entschieden zum Bewußtsein kommen; der 2. Satz schlug sehr durch; der Schlußsatz entzündete großen Jubel", so berichtet Alfred Dörffel in den *Leipziger Nachrichten* über die Reaktion des Premieren-Publikums, und die Musikkritik war sich hier wie auch dann bei der Wiener Erstaufführung am 14. Januar 1879 einig, dass dieses Violinkonzert von Brahms „das bedeutendste heißen [darf], was seit dem Beethovenschen und Mendelssohnschen erschien". Dabei gehörte zu jenem ‚Bedeutendsten' vor allem die sinfonische Ausrichtung des Konzerts: Das Soloinstrument dominiert nicht, steht mit seinem Können nicht im Vordergrund, sondern verschmilzt im Sinne eines übergeordneten musikalisch Gemeinsamen ganz und gar mit dem Orchester. Hoch virtuos aber gebärdet sich die Solostimme dabei trotzdem mit ihren Doppelgriffen, ihren schnellen Saitenwechseln und ihren Läufen. Doch sind sie nicht virtuoser Selbstzweck, sondern fest eingebunden in die thematische Darbietung, Verarbeitung und Entwicklung eines sinfonischen Ganzen mit all der Ausdrucksvielfalt der musikalischen Sprache des Pörtschacher Brahms: Sinnierendes steht neben Serenadenhaftem, neben „Gartenmusik" und Pastoralem, neben Ernstem erklingt Spielerisches und Witziges (Satz III: *Allegro giocoso*); und über allem herrscht wie in der ein Jahr zuvor in Pörtschach entstandenen 2. Sinfonie jene unbeschwert freundliche Stimmung „voller Sonnenschein".

Klaus Döge

Joseph Joachim zugeeignet

Violin Concerto

Johannes Brahms
(1833–1897)
Op. 77

I. Allegro non troppo

12
Fl. 1 2
a 2
a 2
Ob. 1 2
Cl. (A) 1 2
Fg. 1 2
a 2
(D) 1 2
Cor.
(E) 3 4
Tr. (D) 1 2
Timp.
Vl. Solo
I
Vl.
II
Vla.
Vc.
Cb.

25
Fl. 1 2
Ob. 1 2
Cl. (A) 1 2
Fg. 1 2
a 2
(D) 1 2
Cor.
(E) 3 4
a 2
Tr. (D) 1 2
Timp.
Vl. Solo
I
Vl.
II
Vla.
Vc.
Cb.
ff
f
tr
8va

A
38
Fl. 1 2
Ob. 1 2
Cl. (A) 1 2
Fg. 1 2
a 2
1.
p
poco cresc.
p cresc.
fp
Cor. (D) 1 2
Cor. (E) 3 4
Tr. (D) 1 2
Timp.
Vl. Solo
Vl. I
Vl. II
Vla.
Vc.
Cb.
(8va)
div.
unis.

50
Fl. 1
Ob. 1
Cl. (A) 1
Fg. 1
(D) 1 2
Cor.
(E) 3 4
Tr. (D) 1 2
Timp.
Vl. Solo
I
Vl.
II
Vla.
Vc.
Cb.
1.
div.
tr
pp
ppp
p

65
Fl. 1
Ob. 1 2
Cl. (A) 1
Fg. 1
(D) 1 2
Cor.
(E) 3 4
Tr. (D) 1 2
Vl. I
Vla.
Vc.
Cb.
dolce
p dolce
p
dim.
78
Vl.
I
II
f marc.
f

B
84
a 2
Fl. 1 2
Ob. 1 2
Cl. (A) 1 2
Fg. 1 2
f
(D) 1 2
Cor.
(E) 3 4
Tr. (D) 1 2
I
Vl.
II
Vla.
Vc.
Cb.
90
fpp
Timp.
tr
Vl. Solo
f marc.

97
Cor. (D) 1 2
cresc.
Timp.
(tr)
cresc.
Vl. Solo
I
Vl.
II
fp
Vla.
102
Fl. 1 2
Ob. 1
Cl. (A) 1 2
Fg. 1 2
Cor. (D) 1 2
Tr. (D) 1 2
Timp.
tr
fpp
f
p
Vc.
fpp
Cb.

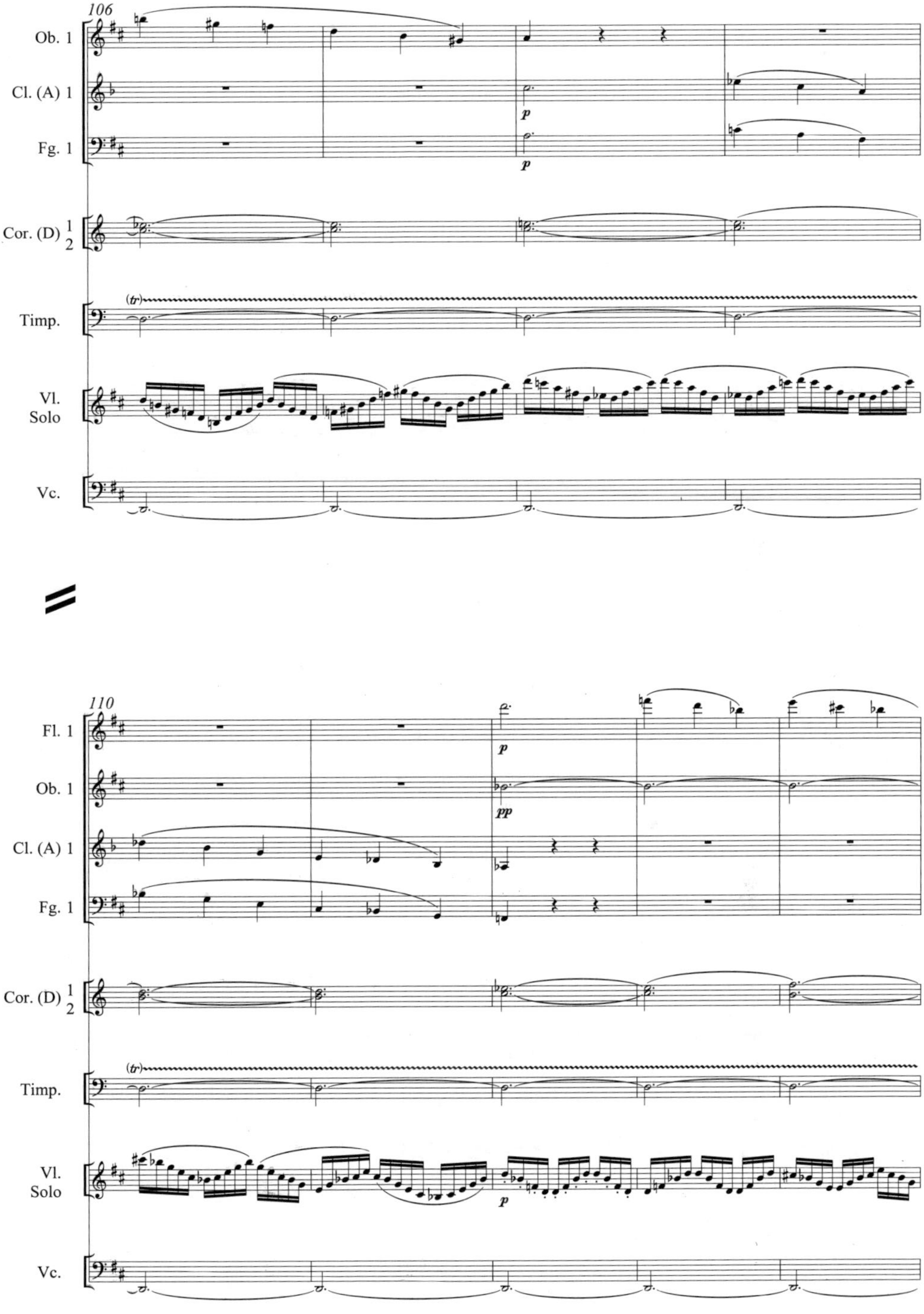

110
Fl. 1
Ob. 1
Cl. (A) 1
Fg. 1
Cor. (D) 1 2
Timp.
(tr)
Vl. Solo
Vc.
p
pp
p

115
1.
Fl. 1 2
Ob. 1
Cl. (A) 1 2
Fg. 1
p
dim.
pp
Cor. (D) 1 2
dim.
Tr. (D) 1 2
(tr)
tr
Timp.
Vl. Solo
Vl. I II
Vla.
Vc.
Cb.
121
muta D in E
espr.

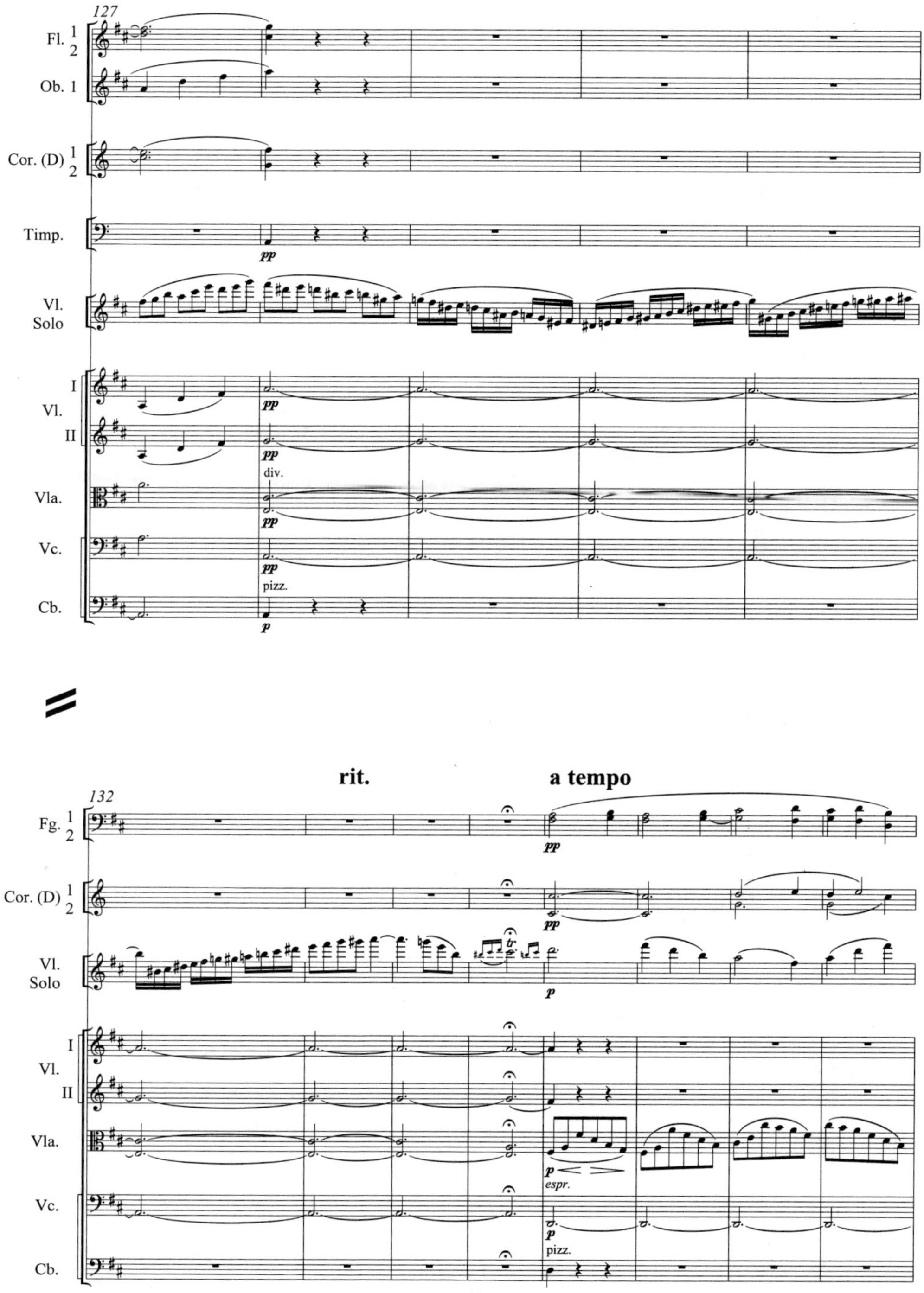

127
Fl. 1 2
Ob. 1
Cor. (D) 1 2
Timp.
pp
Vl. Solo
I
Vl.
II
pp
pp
div.
Vla.
pp
Vc.
pp
pizz.
Cb.
p
rit.
a tempo
132
Fg. 1 2
pp
Cor. (D) 1 2
pp
Vl. Solo
tr
p
I
Vl.
II
Vla.
p
espr.
Vc.
p
pizz.
Cb.

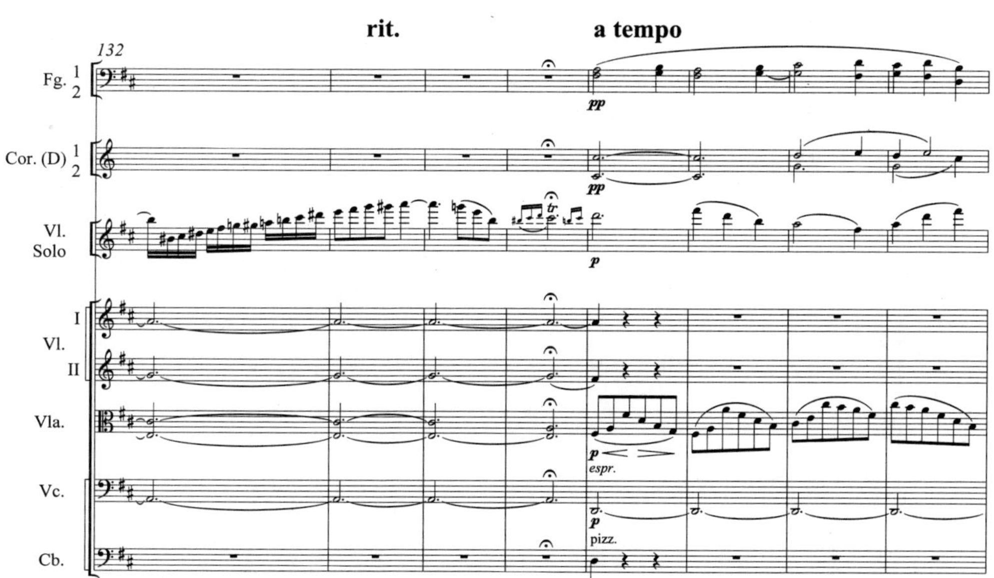

140
Fg. 1 2
Cor. (D) 1 2
Vl. Solo
tr
I
Vl.
II
p
Vla.
Vc.
Cb.

148
(D) 1 2
Cor.
(E) 3 4
p
Vl. Solo
tr
8va
dolce
I
Vl.
II
Vla.
Vc.
Cb.
espr.
arco
p dolce

158
Fg. 2
p
f
(D) 1 2
Cor.
(E) 3 4
f
Vl. Solo
cresc.
f
I
Vl.
II
f
f
Vla.
espr.
cresc.
f
Vc.
cresc.
fp marc.
Cb.
cresc.
fp marc.
165
Vl. Solo
I
Vl.
II
mf marc.
mf marc.
Vla.
mf marc.
Vc.
mf
Cb.
mf
C
172
Vl. Solo
I
Vl.
II
f
f
Vla.
f
Vc.
f
Cb.
f

178
fp
Fl. 1 2
Fg. 1 2
p
Cor. (E) 3 4
fp
Vl. Solo
p dolce
I
Vl.
II
Vla.
Vc.

184
Cl. (A) 1
Fg. 1
pp
Cor. (E) 3 4
Vl. Solo
cresc.
I
Vl.
II
Vla.
Vc.

190
Fl. 1
Cl. (A) 1
Fg. 1
Vl. Solo
I
Vl.
II
Vla.
Vc.
Cb.
197
Fl. 1 2
Ob. 1 2
Cl. (A) 1
Fg. 1
(D) 1 2
Cor.
(E) 3 4
Timp.
Vl. Solo
I
Vl.
II
Vla.
Vc.
Cb.
div.
div.

D
206
Cl. (A) 1
Fg. 1 2
Cor. (D) 1
Vl. Solo
Vl. I II
Vla.
Vc.
Cb.
p
2.
pizz.
p dolce
arco
dolce
215
Fl. 1
Ob. 1
Cl. (A) 1
Fg. 1 2
(D) 1 Cor. (E) 3
Vl. Solo
Vl. I II
Vla.
Vc.
Cb.
dim.
pizz.
0

224
Fl. 1
Cl. (A) 1 2
Fg. 1 2
(D) 1
Cor.
(E) 3 4
Vl. Solo
dolce lusingando
Vl. I
Vl. II
Vla.
Vc.
Cb.
pizz.
p
pp
dim.
233
arco
div.
dim.
pp dim.
246
f
mf

252
Vl.
Solo
I
Vl.
II
Vla.
Vc.
Cb.
mf
257
Fl. 1 2
Ob. 1 2
Cl. (A) 1 2
Fg. 1 2
(D) 1 2
Cor.
(E) 3 4
ff
f
262
cresc.

E
268
Fl. 1 2
Ob. 1 2
Cl. (A) 1 2
Fg. 1 2
(D) 1 2
Cor.
(E) 3 4
Tr. (D) 1 2
Timp.
Vl. Solo
I
Vl.
II
Vla.
Vc.
Cb.

274
Fl. 1 2
Ob. 1 2
Cl. (A) 1 2
Fg. 1 2
a 2
(D) 1 2
Cor.
(E) 3 4
Tr. (D) 1 2
Timp.
(tr)
tr
Vl. Solo
I
Vl.
II
Vla.
Vc.
Cb.

283
Fl. 1 2
Ob. 1 2
Cl. (A) 1 2
Fg. 1 2
(D) 1 2
Cor.
(E) 3 4
Tr. (D) 1 2
Timp.
Vl. I II
Vla.
Vc.
Cb.
a 2
(tr)
E muta in D
pizz.
pf
p
1.
292
Fl. 1
Ob. 1
Cl. (A) 1 2
Fg. 1 2
Cor. (D) 1 2
arco
mp
pp
2.

302
Cl. (A) 1 2
dim.
Fg. 1 2
dim.
Vl. Solo
poco f espr.
Vl. II
arco
p
Vla.
dim.
pizz.
arco
Vc.
dim.
p
pizz.
Cb.
dim.
p
tranquillo
312
Ob. 1
p dolce
Cl. (A) 1
p
p
Fg. 1 2
p
Vl. Solo
p legg. ma espr. (grazioso)
simile
Vl. II
Vla.
pizz.
arco
Vc.
319
Fg. 1 2
Vl. Solo
I
Vl.
II
p
p
Vla.
p
Vc.
p

326
poco rit.
Vl. Solo
Vl. I
Vl. II
Vla.
Vc.
dim.
ppp
332
a tempo
f cresc.
f
mf marc.
cresc.
mf cresc.
Cb.
339
F
Fl. 1 2
Ob. 1 2
Cl. (A) 1 2
Fg. 1 2
Cor. (D) 1 2
a 2
f marc.

344
Fl. 1 2
Ob. 1 2
Cl. (A) 1 2
Fg. 1 2
(D) 1 2
Cor.
(E) 3 4
Tr. (D) 1 2
Vl. Solo
I
Vl.
II
Vla.
Vc.
Cb.
a 2
ff
fp
f
più f
fp marc.
div.
351
cresc.
p cresc.
mf cresc.
8va

360
Fl. 1 2
mf
Ob. 1 2
mf
Cl. (A) 1 2
mf
Fg. 1 2
mf
(D) 1 2
Cor.
(E) 3 4
Tr. (D) 1 2
Timp.
tr
pp
Vl. Solo
f
I
Vl.
II
Vla.
Vc.
Cb.
trem.
fpp

367
Fl. 1 2
Ob. 1 2
Cl. (A) 1 2
Fg. 1 2
(D) 1 2
Cor.
(E) 3 4
Tr. (D) 1 2
Timp.
Vl. Solo
I
Vl.
II
Vla.
Vc.
Cb.
p cresc.
fp
tr

poco rit.
375
Fl. 1 2
Ob. 1 2
Cl. (A) 1 2
Fg. 1 2
(D) 1 2
Cor.
(E) 3 4
Tr. (D) 1 2
Timp.
Vl. Solo
I
Vl.
II
Vla.
Vc.
Cb.
fp
f
p
cresc.
sf
(tr)
tr

G a tempo
381
Fl. 1 2
Ob. 1 2
Cl. (A) 1 2
Fg. 1 2
(D) 1 2
Cor.
(E) 3 4
Tr. (D) 1 2
Timp.
Vl. Solo
I
Vl.
II
Vla.
Vc.
Cb.
ff
f
fp dim.
a 2
tr
p
pizz.

390
Fl. 1
Ob. 1 2
Cl. (A) 1 2
(D) 1 2
Cor.
(E) 3 4
Vl. Solo
Vl. I
Vl. II
Vla.
Vc.
Cb.
pp
p
1.
3.
p dolce
8va
dolce
arco
399
p dolce
dolce
cresc.
f
fp marc.

407
Vl.
Solo
Vl.
I
II
Vla.
Vc.
Cb.
mf marc.
pizz.
414
H
f
419
Ob. 1 2
Cl. (A) 1 2
Fg. 1 2
fp
p
div.
1.

425
Fl. 1
Ob. 1
Cor. (D) 1 2
Vl. Solo
poco cresc.
Vl. I
Vl. II
div.
Vla.
Vc.
Cb.
arco
432
Cl. (A) 1 2
Fg. 1
(D) 1 2 Cor. (E) 3 4
Timp.
tr

I
441
Fl. 1 2
Ob. 1 2
Cl. (A) 1 2
Fg. 1 2
(D) 1
Cor.
(E) 3
Vl. Solo
Vl. I
Vla.
Vc.
Cb.
pp
p
1.
2.
dolce
pizz.
450
Cl. (A) 1
(D) 1 2
Cor.
(E) 3 4
Vl.
I
II
mp
mf
p dolce
arco

459
Fl. 1 2
Ob. 1
Cl. (A) 1
Fg. 1 2
Cor. (D) 1 2
Vl. Solo
Vl. I II
Vla.
Vc.
Cb.
1.
2.
p
dim.
espr.
p lusingando
pizz.
arco
468
Cl. (A) 1 2
(D) 1 2
Cor.
(E) 3 4
pp

477
K
Vl.
Solo
arco
I
Vl.
II
Vla.
Vc.
Cb.
p
pp
dim.
f
489
494
mf

499

Fl. 1 2
Ob. 1 2
Cl. (A) 1 2
Fg. 1 2
Cor. (D) 1 2
Vl. Solo
I Vl. II
Vla.
Vc.
Cb.

ff mf

509
Fl. 1 2
Ob. 1 2
Cl. (A) 1 2
Fg. 1 2
(D) 1 2
Cor.
(E) 3 4
Tr. (D) 1 2
Timp.
Vl. Solo
I
Vl.
II
Vla.
Vc.
Cb.
fp
f
8va

513
Fl. 1 2
ff
Ob. 1 2
Cl. (A) 1 2
Fg. 1 2
a 2
(D) 1 2
Cor.
f
(E) 3 4
Tr. (D) 1 2
tr
Timp.
Vl. Solo
I
Vl.
II
Vla.
Vc.
Cb.

522
tranquillo
Fl. 1 2
Ob. 1 2
Cl. (A) 1 2
a 2
1.
Fg. 1 2
pp
(D) 1 2
Cor.
(E) 3 4
pp
Tr. (D) 1 2
tr
Timp.
Cadenza
tr
Vl. Solo
p dolce
8va
I
Vl.
II
pp
pp
Vla.
pp
Vc.
pp
pizz.
Cb.
pp

535
Fl. 1
dolce
pp
Ob. 1
dolce
p dolce
Cl. (A) 1 2
1.
dolce
pp
Fg. 1 2
(D) 1 2
pp
p
Cor.
(E) 3
dolce
Tr. (D) 1 2
Timp.
(8va)
Vl. Solo
espr.
dim.
dolce
I
Vl.
II
pp
dim.
Vla.
Vc.
Cb.
arco
pizz.

548
Fl. 1 2
Cl. (A) 1 2
Cor. (D) 1 2
Vl. Solo
poco a poco cresc.
I
Vl.
II
Vla.
Vc.
Cb.
string. poco a poco
animato
554
Fg. 1 2
p cresc.
cresc.
Tr. (D) 1 2
Timp.
f
p
fp

560
Fl. 1 2
Ob. 1 2
Cl. (A) 1 2
Fg. 1 2
(D) 1 2
Cor.
(E) 3 4
p
cresc.
Tr. (D) 1 2
cresc.
Timp.
cresc.
Vl. Solo
I
Vl.
II
cresc.
Vla.
cresc.
Vc.
Cb.
cresc.

565
Fl. 1 2
Ob. 1 2
Cl. (A) 1 2
Fg. 1 2
(D) 1 2
Cor.
(E) 3 4
Tr. (D) 1 2
Timp.
Vl. Solo
I
Vl.
II
Vla.
Vc.
Cb.
mf
f
tr

II. Adagio

Flauto 1 2

p

Oboe 1 2

1.

dolce

Clarinetto (B♭) 1 2

p

Fagotto 1 2

p

Corno (F) 1 2

p

Violino Solo

Violino I

Violino II

Viola

Violoncello

Contrabbasso

17
Fl. 1 2
Ob. 1
Cl. (B♭) 1 2
Fg. 1 2
Cor. (F) 1 2
pp
dim.
p
26
Fl. 1
Ob. 1 2
Cl. (B♭) 1 2
Fg. 1 2
Cor. (F) 1 2
Vl. Solo
I
Vl.
II
Vla.
Vc.
Cb.
mf
p dolce

34
Fl. 1
Cl. (B♭) 1
Fg. 1
Cor. (F) 1
Vl.
Solo
I
Vl.
II
Vla.
Vc.
Cb.
p
41
1.
Fl. 1 2
Ob. 1
Cl. (B♭) 1 2
Fg. 1 2
Cor. (F) 1 2
p cresc.
p dolce
p poco cresc.
dolce p
pizz.
arco

48
Fl. 1 2
Ob. 1 2
Cl. (B♭) 1 2
Fg. 1 2
Cor. (F) 1 2
a 2
Vl. Solo
I
Vl.
II
Vla.
Vc.
Cb.
arco
poco a poco più largamente
54
mf cresc.
cresc.
f espr.
poco f

60
Fl. 1
Cl. (B♭) 1 2
Fg. 1
Vl. Solo
I
Vl.
II
Vla.
Vc.
p
poco

64
Vl. Solo
I
Vl.
II
Vla.
Vc.
p

69
Vl.
Solo
cresc.
I
Vl.
II
cresc.
Vla.
cresc.
Vc.
cresc.
Cb.
cresc.

73
calando
Fg. 2
dim.
Cor. (F) 1 2
p dim.
Vl.
Solo
8va
dim.
dolce
I
Vl.
II
dim. molto
Vla.
dim. molto
Vc.
dim. molto
Cb.
dim. molto

Tempo I
78
Fl. 1
Ob. 1
dolce
Cl. (B♭) 1 2
pp
Fg. 1 2
2.
pp
Cor. (F) 1 2
1.
Vl. Solo
(8va)
dolce
I
Vl.
II
ppp
Vla.
Vc.
Cb.
p
84
Ob. 1 2
Cl. (B♭) 1 2
Fg. 1 2
Cor. (F) 1 2
Vl. Solo
espr.
pp

90
Fl. 1 2
1.
poco a poco cresc.
mp
Ob. 1 2
1.
cresc.
Cl. (B♭) 1 2
poco a poco cresc.
Fg. 1 2
cresc.
Cor. (F) 1 2
espr.
poco a poco cresc.
Vl. Solo
espr.
poco a poco cresc.
I
Vl.
II
pizz.
poco a poco cresc.
Vla.
Vc.
Cb.

96
Fl. 1 2
Ob. 1
Cl. (B♭) 1 2
Fg. 2
Cor. (F) 1 2
Vl. Solo
espr. dolce
I
Vl.
II
Vla.
Vc.
Cb.

103
Ob. 1
Cl. (B♭) 1 2
dolce
Fg. 1 2
1.
p dolce
Cor. (F) 1 2
p
pp
Vl. Solo
p
dolce
p
I
Vl.
II
arco
pp
arco
pp
Vla.
arco
pp
Vc.
pp
Cb.
pp
109
Fl. 1 2
pp
pp
Ob. 1 2
pp
Cl. (B♭) 1 2
pp
Fg. 1 2
pp
Cor. (F) 1 2
pp
Vl. Solo
pp
p
dim.
dim.
dim.
dim.
dim.
pp
Vla.
Vc.
Cb.

III. Allegro giocoso, ma non troppo vivace

6
Fl. 1 2
Ob. 1 2
Cl. (A) 1 2
Fg. 1 2
(D) 1 2
Cor.
(E) 3 4
Tr. (D) 1 2
Timp.
Vl. Solo
I
Vl.
II
Vla.
Vc.
Cb.
f ben marc.
sf
f
6

12
A
1.
Fl. 1 2
Ob. 1 2
Cl. (A) 1 2
Fg. 1 2
(D) 1 2
Cor.
(E) 3 4
Timp.
Vl. Solo
Vl. I
Vl. II
Vla.
Vc.
Cb.
pizz.
p
18
Fl. 1
Ob. 1
Cl. (A) 1
Fg. 1
Cor. (D) 1
tr

25
Fl. 1 2
Ob. 1 2
Cl. (A) 1 2
Fg. 1 2
(D) 1 2
Cor.
(E) 3 4
Tr. (D) 1 2
Timp.
Vl. Solo
I
Vl.
II
Vla.
Vc.
Cb.
cresc.
tr
f
marc.
sf
a 2
ff
arco
div.

33
Fl. 1 2
Ob. 1 2
Cl. (A) 1 2
Fg. 1 2
(D) 1 2
Cor.
(E) 3 4
Tr. (D) 1 2
Timp.
Vl. Solo
I
Vl.
II
Vla.
Vc.
Cb.
f
p
sf
p legg.

40
Vl. Solo
I
Vl.
II
Vla.
Vc.
Cb.
legg.
legg.
legg.
legg.
pizz.
45
Vl. Solo
I
Vl.
II
Vla.
Vc.
Cb.
50
Vl. Solo
cresc.
pizz.
I
f
cresc.
Vl.
pizz.
II
f
cresc.
pizz.
Vla.
f
cresc.
pizz.
Vc.
f
cresc.

B
55
Fl. 1 2
Ob. 1 2
Cl. (A) 1 2
Fg. 1 2
(D) 1 2 Cor. (E) 3 4
Vl. Solo
ff energicamente
I Vl. II
arco
Vla.
arco
ff marc.
Vc.
arco
Cb.
pizz.
arco
pizz.
62
a 2
arco

71
C
Fl. 1 2
Ob. 1 2
Cl. (A) 1 2
Fg. 1 2
a 2
ff
(D) 1 2
Cor.
(E) 3 4
Tr. (D) 1 2
Timp.
Vl. Solo
8va
I
Vl.
II
Vla.
Vc.
Cb.

79
Fl. 1 2
Ob. 1 2
Cl. (A) 1 2
Fg. 1 2
(D) 1 2
Cor.
(E) 3 4
Tr. (D) 1 2
Timp.
Vl. Solo
I
Vl.
II
Vla.
Vc.
Cb.
a 2

90
Fl. 1 2
Ob. 1 2
Cl. (A) 1 2
Fg. 1 2
a 2
(D) 1 2
Cor.
(E) 3 4
Tr. (D) 1 2
Timp.
tr
Vl. Solo
f
sf
I
Vl.
II
Vla.
Vc.
Cb.
mf

98
Fl. 1 2
Ob. 1 2
Cl. (A) 1 2
Fg. 1 2
(D) 1 2
Cor.
(E) 3 4
Tr. (D) 1 2
Timp.
Vl. Solo
I
Vl.
II
Vla.
Vc.
Cb.

105

D

Fl. 1 2

Ob. 1 2

Cl. (A) 1 2

Fg. 1 2

(D) 1 2 Cor. (E) 3 4

Vl. Solo

I Vl. II

Vla.

Vc.

Cb.

f

p

a 2

mf

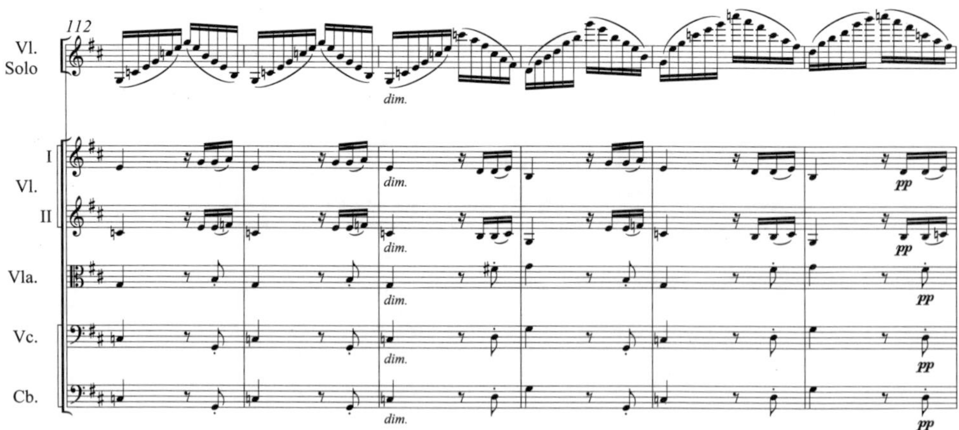

118
Vl.
Solo
p dolce
teneramente
I
Vl.
II
p dolce
p
Vla.
p dolce
pizz.
Vc.
p dolce
pizz.
Cb.
p dolce

124
Fl. 1 2
pp
Ob. 1
p dolce
più p
Cl. (A) 1 2
pp
Fg. 1 2
pp
1.
pp
Cor. (E) 3 4
pp dolce
Vl.
Solo
6
dolce
I
Vl.
II
pp
pp
Vla.
pp
arco
Vc.
pp
pizz.
arco
Cb.
pp
pizz.

130
Fl. 1
dolce
Ob. 1
Cl. (A) 1
dolce
Fg. 1
(D) 1 2
Cor.
(E) 3
pp
pp
Vl.
Solo
I
Vl.
II
pp
pp
Vla.
pp
arco
Vc.
pp
Cb.
E
134
Fl. 1
p
Cl. (A) 1 2
p
Fg. 1
p
(D) 1 2
Cor.
(E) 3
Vl.
Solo
cresc.
espr.
I
Vl.
II
p
p
Vla.
p
più p
Vc.
p
arco
più p
Cb.
p
più p

139
1.
a 2
Fl. 1 2
Ob. 1 2
Cl. (A) 1 2
Fg. 1 2
Cor. (D) 1 2
Vl. Solo
I
Vl.
II
Vla.
Vc.
Cb.
sf
f
mf
pizz.
cresc.
145
Cor. (E) 3 4
Tr. (D) 1 2

F
150
Fl. 1 2
Ob. 1 2
Cl. (A) 1 2
Fg. 1 2
(D) 1 2
Cor.
(E) 3 4
a 2
Tr. (D) 1 2
a 2
Vl. Solo
I
Vl.
II
arco
Vla.
ff marc.
Vc.
arco
Cb.
pizz.
158
Fg. 1 2
(D) 1 2
Cor.
(E) 3 4
Vl. Solo
8va
I
Vl.
II
Vla.
Vc.
Cb.
arco

G
166
Fl. 1 2
Ob. 1 2
Cl. (A) 1 2
Fg. 1 2
(D) 1 2
Cor.
(E) 3 4
Tr. (D) 1 2
Timp.
Vl. Solo
I
Vl.
II
Vla.
Vc.
Cb.

175
Fl. 1 2
a 2
ff
Ob. 1 2
Cl. (A) 1 2
Fg. 1 2
(D) 1 2
Cor.
(E) 3 4
Tr. (D) 1 2
f
Timp.
Vl. Solo
6
I
Vl.
II
Vla.
Vc.
Cb.

184
Fl. 1
Ob. 1
Cl. (A) 1 2
Fg. 1 2
(D) 1 2
Cor.
(E) 3 4
Tr. (D) 1 2
Vl. Solo
I
Vl.
II
Vla.
Vc.
Cb.
a 2
pizz.
tr
191
arco

H
199
Fl. 1 2
Ob. 1 2
Cl. (A) 1 2
Fg. 1 2
(D) 1 2
Cor.
(E) 3 4
Tr. (D) 1 2
Timp.
Vl. Solo
I
Vl.
II
Vla.
Vc.
Cb.
cresc.
mf cresc.
p cresc.
f ben marc.
f
sf
tr

206
Fl. 1 2
Ob. 1 2
Cl. (A) 1 2
Fg. 1 2
(D) 1 2
Cor.
(E) 3 4
Tr. (D) 1 2
Timp.
Vl. Solo
I
Vl.
II
Vla.
Vc.
Cb.
sf
cresc.
a 2
tr
marc.

213
Fl. 1 2
Ob. 1 2
Cl. (A) 1 2
Fg. 1 2
(D) 1 2
Cor.
(E) 3 4
Tr. (D) 1 2
Timp.
Vl. Solo
I
Vl.
II
Vla.
Vc.
Cb.

219
Fl. 1 2
Ob. 1 2
Cl. (A) 1 2
Fg. 1 2
(D) 1 2
Cor.
(E) 3 4
Tr. (D) 1 2
Timp.
Vl. Solo
(8va)
f
I
Vl.
II
mp
cresc.
Vla.
Vc.
Cb.
229
I
1.
p
ff
legg.
tr
sf
ppp
pizz.
Cor. (D) 1 2

236
Fl. 1 2
Ob. 1 2
Cl. (A) 1 2
Fg. 1 2
Cor. (D) 1 2
Vl. Solo
più p
I
Vl.
II
pizz.
Vla.
Vc.
244
Cor. (D) 2
arco
Cb.

250
Vl. Solo
I
Vl.
II
Vla.
Vc.
Cb.
cresc.
255
Cor. (D) 1 2
p marc.
cresc.
cresc.
Timp.
p
cresc.
cresc.
Vl. Solo
f
energicamente
sf
I
Vl.
II
Vla.
Vc. Cb.
p
263
Fl. 1 2
p
f
Ob. 1 2
p
f
Cl. (A) 1 2
p
f
Fg. 1 2
p
f
(D) 1 2
Cor.
(E) 3 4
f
Tr. (D) 1 2
f
Timp.
tr
f
Vl. Solo
sf
sf
I
Vl.
II
Vla.
Vc. Cb.
f

267
Poco più presto
Fl. 1
Ob. 1
Cl. (A) 1
Fg. 1
Timp.
Vl.
Solo
I
Vl.
II
Vla.
Vc.
Cb.
p
pp
p cresc.
cresc.
p ma ben marc.
leggiero
pizz.
K
275
a 2
Fl.
Ob.
Cl. (A)
Fg.
Cor. (D)
Tr. (D)
f
mf
pp
pp legg.
legg.
arco
legg.
pizz.

283
Fl. 1 2
Ob. 1 2
Cl. (A) 1 2
Fg. 1 2
Cor. (D) 1 2
Tr. (D) 1 2
Timp.
Vl. Solo
I Vl. II
Vla.
Vc.
Cb.
cresc.
a 2
f
arco
290
Fl. 1
Ob. 1
Cor. (D) 1
p
pp legg.
pizz.
pp
dim.
1.

L
298
Fl. 1 2
Ob. 1 2
Cor. (D) 1 2
Timp.
Vl. Solo
I
Vl.
II
Vla.
Vc.
Cb.
1.
dolce
pp
a 2
p
p leggiero
legg.
pizz.
arco
306
cresc.
Cl. (A) 1 2
Fg. 1 2
Tr. (D) 1 2
f

315
Ob. 1 2
Cl. (A) 1 2
Fg. 1 2
Vl. Solo
Vl. I II
Vla.
Vc.
Cb.
pizz.
arco
cresc.
M
323
Fl. 1 2
(D) 1 2
Cor.
(E) 3 4
Tr. (D) 1 2
Timp.

331
Fl. 1 2
Ob. 1 2
Cl. (A) 1 2
Fg. 1 2
a 2
ff
f cresc.
(D) 1 2
Cor.
(E) 3 4
Tr. (D) 1 2
Timp.
Vl. Solo
I
Vl.
II
Vla.
Vc.
Cb.
p
f
sf

Printed in China

THE ART OF SCORE-READING

The first steps

A score contains the entire musical text of a musical work in order that the conductor and everyone who wants to study the piece more thoroughly can see exactly which passages are being played by the orchestra or ensemble. The parts of the individual instruments are arranged in such a way that all notes played at the same time are written one below the other.
Scores help to listen to, understand and interpret musical works. Those who only listen to music are unaware of many important details which, after some practice, become apparent when reading the score while listening to the music. The clear structure of the score helps to easily understand the compositional style and the characteristic features of a piece – this is a prerequisite not only for any analysis but also for the musician's own performance and interpretation.

The simplest method of score-reading is to read an individual part by concentrating on an individual part that can be heard particularly well. The most suitable pieces to begin with are concertos with solo instruments such as Beethoven's Romance in F major for violin and orchestra (example 1) or orchestral songs (with them, one may easily follow the text). Furthermore, in many classical orchestral works, it is quite easy to follow the lead part of the principal violin, or the bass part in baroque compositions for orchestra.

The next step is to try to change from one part to another and vice versa and follow the part that is leading. Little by little, you learn to find distinctive parts you hear in the score as well and follow them in the corresponding staff. This can be very easily tried out with Beethoven's Symphony No. 5 (example 2). To read the score, it is also helpful to count the bars. This technique is rather useful in the case of confusing or complex scores, such as those of contemporary music, and is particularly suitable when you do not want to lag behind in any case. It should be your aim, however, to eventually give up counting the bars and to read the score by first following individual parts and then going over to section-by-section or selective reading (see next page).

Example 1 · from: Romance for violin and orchestra in F major by Beethoven

Example 2 · from: Symphony No. 5 C-minor by Beethoven

Further score-reading techniques

Example 3 · from: Symphony No. 100 G major 'Military' by Haydn

Example 4 · from: Symphony No. 41 C major 'Jupiter' by W. A. Mozart

Section-by-section reading

This technique is suitable for application in the 'Military' Symphony by Haydn (example 3). In bb. 260-264, the parts are mostly in parallel motion so that it is quite easy to take in the section as a whole. In the strings, the texture is homophonic (i.e. all instruments play the same rhythm), consisting of tone repetitions in the lower parts while there is a little more movement in the part of the first violin. At the same time, the tones of the winds are stationary (i.e. long sustained notes), serving as harmonic filling-in. If need be, they can also be read en bloc.

Such block-like structures often consist of unison figures (= all instruments play the same), such as at the beginning of Mozart's Jupiter Symphony (example 4). Here, the score-reading can first be limited to the strings section which carries the melody alone in bb. 3-4 and contains all important information.

Example 5 · from: Symphony No. 7 A major by Beethoven

Selektive reading

Using this technique, you concentrate on selected parts (lead parts, conspicuous passages) in the score. In the excerpt from Beethoven's Symphony No. 7 (example 5), it is the semiquaver motif that, originating with the violoncellos and basses and pervading the string parts twice, is particularly well suited. The stationary tones of the winds, consisting only of the note E in various octave positions in bb. 358-363, form the harmonic foundation and play a subordinate role in score-reading. Though they are briefly noticed, it is the strings and especially the conspicuous semiquaver motif pervading the individual parts that are to be followed.

With both score-reading techniques which should be chosen according to the nature of the passage in question, it is not important in the beginning to be able to follow at once all tones and harmonies. What matters more is to recognize and comprehend sequences of movement. Everything else comes with experience.

Following contrapuntal parts

The present excerpt from Brahms's Requiem (example 6) is polyphonic, i.e. one has to be able to follow several equal parts either alternately (without lagging behind) or simultaneously. But by looking for parallel parts in the score, the notation which, at first glance, seems to be overcrowded soon becomes clearer. For example, Brahms allocates orchestral parts to each choral part. As a consequence, there are many parts written in the score but considerably fewer independent parts actually played. Hence, the large amount of written music can be reduced to a manageable quantity.

The flute, clarinet, first violins and soprano are in parallel motion. Furthermore, the tenor of oboe and viola is supported by a much-expanded, yet parallel part.
The violoncellos and bassoons too are in almost parallel motion.

The low winds and strings as well as the timpani played simultaneously with the polyphonic parts are fill-in parts which consist only of stationary tones (sustained notes). They do not need to be followed upon first reading of the score.

Seen as a whole, this excerpt is most suitable for focussing on the soprano voice as it is coupled with two instruments and, being the highest voice, can be heard very well. In addition, the text is an aid to orientation, making it easier to return from brief trips to other parts.

In fugal sections, score-reading will be easier if the entries of the theme in the score are first looked for and then marked.

Example 6 · from: A German Requiem by Brahms

The score at a glance

A **Bar lines** are solid vertical lines within the instrument sections.

B The **bar numbers** are an aid to orientation in the score. Sometimes capital letters, so-called rehearsal letters, are used instead of numbers.

C The system of parallel lines on and between which the notes are written is called **staff** (or stave). The instrument abbreviation in front of each line (here, Fl. is for 'flute') indicates to which instrument(s) the line(s) refer(s).

D The **barline at the left-hand end** of the staves connects all staves to form the **system**.

E In addition to the barline at the left-hand end of the staves, **angular brackets** connect the individual groups of instruments in a score (wind, brass and string instruments). Within these groups, the instruments are arranged according to their pitch, with the highest-pitched instrument mentioned first.
Today, the common order of instrumental parts in the score is as follows, from top to bottom:

· wind instruments
· brass instruments
· percussion instruments
· harp, piano, celesta
· solo instrument(s)
· solo voices
· choir
· string instruments

F When there are two systems on a page, they are separated from each other by two parallel **diagonal strokes**.

G Instruments the names of which are followed by 'in Bb' or (Bb) are **transposing instruments**. In this case, (Bb) indicates that the notated C is played as Bb, i.e. all tones are played a tone lower than notated. Most of the transposing instruments are easily recognizable in the score thanks to these additions. However, there are also transposing instruments without such indications in the score, such as:

· piccolo flute (in C / an octave higher)
· cor anglais (in F / a fifth lower)
· contrabassoon (in C / an octave lower)
· double bass (in C / an octave lower)

H The transposing brass instruments have no general signature but, if need be, accidentals preceding the respective tone.

I The viola part is notated in the **alto clef**, the parts of violoncello and bassoon sometimes in the **tenor clef**. Both clefs are easy to read when the player realizes that the clef frames the note C1:

alto clef = tenor clef = treble clef

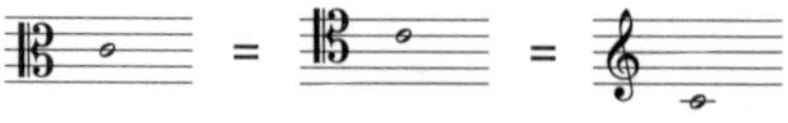

J Any change of key or time is marked by a **double bar**. The alla-breve sign following in this example (¢), like the sign for four-four time (c), is a relic from an old notational practice and stands for two-two time.

B
A
C
4
29
Fl.
Ob.
D
Cl. (B♭)
E
Fag.
Cor. (B♭)
Vl.
I
II
Vla.
Vc.
Cb.
sfp
dim.
pp
arco
F
34
G
H
Tr. (B♭)
Timp.
cresc.
ff
I
J

A
Section-by-section reading:
For parts which, rhythmically, move in parallel motion.
Allegro vivace o 80
B
C
D
Selective reading:
The lead part is followed.
E

from: Symphony No. 4 Bb by Beethoven

A **Tempo indications** (sometimes in connection with metronome markings) are used by the composer to indicate how fast a piece shall be played.

B In the winds, two parts are usually brought together in one line. If they play the same note, the note head either has two stems or 'a2' written above it.

C Two-part chords in the staves of the strings are played by one player. If the parts shall be divided, **divisi** (divided) is written in the score. Then, at each desk, one player plays the upper notes and another player the lower notes.

D When an instrumental part contains a long rest, as in this flute part for example, its staff is often omitted until the next entry of the instrument, thus saving space. In addition, there are less page-turns, and the playing parts are arranged much clearer.

E In order to save space and arrange phrases or groups of notes more clearly, so-called abbreviations are used occasionally. The sign 𝅗𝅥 stands for ♩♩♩♩, with the minim indicating the duration of the repetitions and the stroke crossing the stem indicating the value of the notes to be repeated (1 stroke = quaver, 2 strokes = semiquaver, etc.). Cf. also the viola in b. 43 in which the repeated notes are first written out and then abbreviated.

Score-Reading with pupils and students!

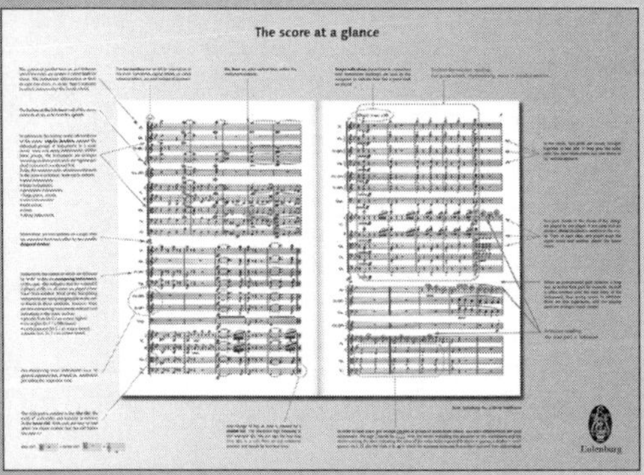

Order this guideline for score-reading for your class! The leaflet 'The Art of Score-Reading' is available separately or as a set of copies and can be obtained free of charge while stock last.

Brochure 'The Art of Score-Reading'

Order No. ETP 9998-99 (free of charge)

Mozart for the classroom

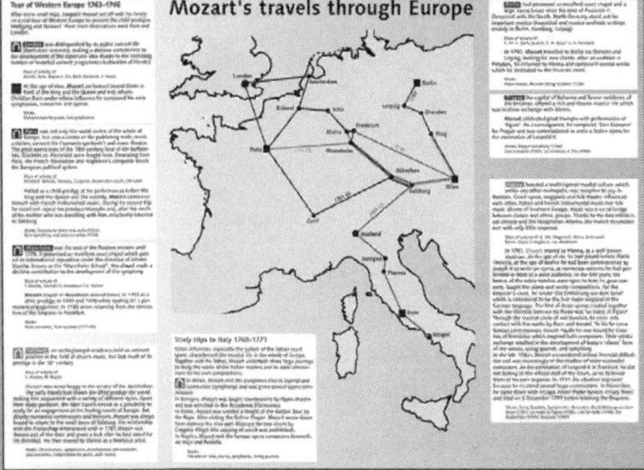

A picture of life and travel

Mozart was not only one of the greatest composers, but also one of the best pianists of the 18th century. Like the virtous of today, he spent a large part of his life on concert tours at the leading courts and great cities of his time.

This small brochure depicts a panorama of the musical life in Europe wich formed the background to Mozart's oeuvre. The picture is completed by a short biography and a little insight into his way of composing.

Brochure 'Mozart. A Picture of Life and Travel'

Order No. ETP 9991-99 (free of charge)

For further information, see at: www.eulenburg.de

Eulenburg

1507 02 MA 06/06

DIE KUNST DES PARTITURLESENS

Der erste Einstieg

Eine Partitur enthält den gesamten Notentext eines Musikwerkes, damit der Dirigent und jeder, der sich näher mit dem Stück beschäftigen will, genau nachvollziehen kann, was das Orchester oder das Ensemble spielt. Dabei sind die Instrumente so angeordnet, dass alle Noten, die zur gleichen Zeit erklingen, genau untereinander stehen. Partituren helfen beim Hören, Begreifen und Interpretieren von Musikliteratur. Wer nur zuhört, erkennt viele kostbare Kleinigkeiten nicht, die beim Mitlesen nach ein wenig Übung regelrecht sichtbar werden. Der Kompositionsstil und die Charakteristik eines Werkes lassen sich mit der übersichtlichen Partitur schnell begreifen – das ist nicht nur Grundvoraussetzung für jede Analyse, sondern auch für das eigene Spiel.

Die einfachste Methode beim Partiturlesen ist das Verfolgen einer Einzelstimme. Bei diesem Verfahren konzentriert man sich auf eine einzelne Stimme, die besonders gut zu hören ist. Zum Einstieg eignen sich dabei besonders gut Konzerte mit Soloinstrumenten wie die Romanze in F-Dur für Violine und Orchester von Beethoven (Beispiel 1) oder Orchesterlieder (bei letzteren kann man sich leicht am Text orientieren). Weiterhin kann man bei vielen klassischen Orchesterwerken die führende Stimme der ersten Violine gut verfolgen, sowie bei barocken Kompositionen für Orchester die Bass-Stimme.

In einem nächsten Schritt kann man versuchen, zwischen den Stimmen zu wechseln und jeweils die Stimme zu verfolgen, die gerade führend ist. Nach und nach lernt man dabei markante Stimmen, die man hört, auch in der Partitur zu finden und im entsprechenden Notensystem zu verfolgen. Besonders anschaulich kann man das mittels Beethovens 5. Symphonie erproben (Beispiel 2).
Eine weitere Hilfe beim Lesen der Partitur kann auch das Mitzählen der Takte sein. Dieses Verfahren hilft bei unübersichtlichen oder komplexen Partituren wie etwa zeitgenössischer Musik und eignet sich besonders, wenn man den Anschluss auf keinen Fall verlieren möchte. Ziel sollte es jedoch sein, das Mitzählen der Takte gänzlich zu verlassen und die Partitur zunächst anhand einzelner Stimmen und dann im Wechsel von blockweisem bzw. selektivem Lesen zu verfolgen (siehe nächste Seite).

Beispiel 1 · aus: Romanze für Violine und Orchester F-Dur von Beethoven

Beispiel 2 · aus: Symphonie Nr. 5 c-moll von Beethoven

Weitere Methoden des Partiturlesens

Beispiel 3 · aus: Symphonie Nr. 100 G-Dur „Militär" von Haydn

Beispiel 4 · aus: Symphonie Nr. 41 C-Dur „Jupiter" von W. A. Mozart

Blockweises Lesen

Diese Methode bietet sich in der Militär-Symphonie von Haydn an (Beispiel 3). In den T. 260-264 sind die Stimmen weitgehend parallel geführt, so dass man sie gut im Ganzen überblicken kann. In den Streichern haben wir einen homophonen Satz (d.h. alle Stimmen spielen den gleichen Rhythmus), der in den unteren Stimmen aus Tonwiederholungen besteht, während die erste Violine etwas bewegter ist. Gleichzeitig erklingen in den Bläserstimmen Liegetöne (d.h. lang ausgehaltene Töne), die als harmonischer Füllstoff dienen. Sie können bei Bedarf auch im Block gelesen werden.
Oft bestehen solche blockhaften Gebilde auch aus unisono-Figuren (= alle Stimmen spielen dasselbe), wie z.B. am Beginn der Jupiter-Symphonie von Mozart (Beispiel 4). Hier kann man sich beim Lesen zunächst nur auf den Streicherblock beschränken, der in den T. 3-4 alleine die Melodie weiterführt und bereits alle wichtigen Informationen enthält.

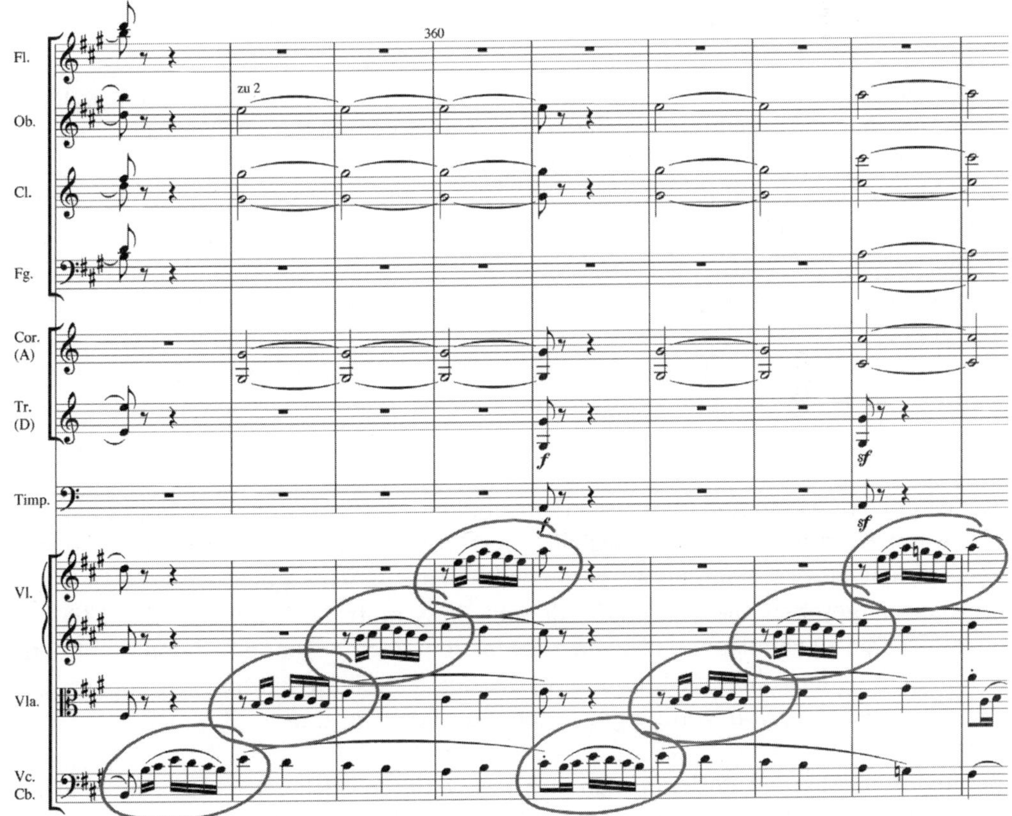

Beispiel 5 · aus: Symphonie Nr. 7 A-Dur von Beethoven

Selektives Lesen

Bei dieser Methode orientiert man sich anhand ausgewählter Stimmen (führende Stimmen, auffällige Stellen) in der Partitur. Im Ausschnitt aus Beethovens 7. Symphonie (Beispiel 5) ist hierzu das Sechzehntelmotiv geeignet, das zweimal von den Celli und Bässen ausgehend durch die Streicherstimmen wandert. Die Liegetöne der Bläser, die in den T. 358-363 sogar nur aus dem Ton e in unterschiedlichen Oktavlagen bestehen, bilden die harmonische Grundierung und spielen beim Lesen der Partitur eine untergeordnete Rolle. Man nimmt sie kurz wahr, verfolgt jedoch die Streicher und dort insbesondere das auffällige Sechzehntelmotiv in seiner Wanderung durch die einzelnen Stimmen.

Bei beiden Leseformen, zwischen denen man übrigens je nach Beschaffenheit der Stelle wechseln sollte, kommt es am Anfang nicht darauf an, sofort alle Töne und Harmonien verfolgen zu können. Viel wichtiger ist es, Bewegungsabläufe zu erkennen und nachzuvollziehen. Alles Weitere kommt mit der Erfahrung.

Verfolgen von kontrapunktischen Stimmen

Der vorliegende Ausschnitt aus Brahms' Requiem (Beispiel 6) ist polyphon komponiert, d.h. man muss mehrere gleichwertige Stimmen entweder im Wechsel (ohne den Anschluss zu verlieren) oder gleichzeitig verfolgen können.

Doch das auf den ersten Blick so übervolle Notenbild lichtet sich bald, wenn man sich die Partitur näher auf parallele Stimmen ansieht. Brahms ordnet z.B. jeder Chorstimme Orchesterstimmen zu. Das hat zur Folge, dass hier zwar viele Stimmen notiert sind, aber wesentlich weniger eigenständige Stimmen tatsächlich erklingen. Die vielen geschriebenen Noten lassen sich also auf ein überschaubares Maß reduzieren.

So werden Flöte, Klarinette, erste Violinen und Sopran parallel geführt. Des Weiteren wird der Tenor von Oboe und Bratsche mit einer stark erweiterten, aber dennoch parallel verlaufenden Stimme unterstützt. Ebenfalls fast ganz parallel verlaufen Violoncelli und Fagotte.

Zu den polyphon gefügten Stimmen erklingen die tiefen Bläser und Streicher sowie die Pauke mit Füllstimmen, welche lediglich aus Liegetönen (ausgehaltene Töne) bestehen. Sie braucht man beim ersten Lesen nicht weiter zu verfolgen.

Im Ganzen gesehen bietet sich in diesem Ausschnitt an, schwerpunktmäßig die Sopranstimme zu verfolgen, da sie mit zwei Instrumenten gekoppelt ist und als höchste Stimme gut herauszuhören ist. Zudem bietet der Text eine Orientierungshilfe, so dass der Wiedereinstieg von vorübergehenden Ausflügen in andere Stimmen erleichtert wird.

Bei fugierten Abschnitten kann man sich das Mitlesen auch erleichtern, indem man zunächst alle Einsätze des Themas in der Partitur sucht und sich markiert.

Beispiel 6 · aus: Ein deutsches Requiem von Brahms

Die Partitur im Überblick

A **Taktstriche** sind innerhalb der Instrumentengruppen durchgezogen.

B Die **Taktzahlen** erleichtern die Orientierung in der Partitur. Manchmal dienen hierzu auch Großbuchstaben, sog. Studierbuchstaben.

C Eine einzelne Zeile der Partitur nennt man **Notensystem**. Für welche(s) Instrument(e) sie steht, zeigt der **Instrumentenvorsatz** an (hier Fl. für Flöte).

D Der **Kopfstrich** verbindet alle Notensysteme miteinander zu einer **Akkolade**.

E Zusätzlich zum Kopfstrich fassen **gerade Klammern** die einzelnen Instrumentengruppen (Holz-, Blech- und Streichinstrumente) zusammen. Innerhalb dieser Gruppen sind die Instrumente nach Tonlage geordnet, wobei das höchste an oberster Stelle steht.
Die heute übliche Partituranordnung lautet von oben nach unten:
· Holzblasinstrumente
· Blechblasinstrumente
· Schlaginstrumente
· Harfe, Klavier, Celesta
· Soloinstrument(e)
· Solostimmen
· Chor
· Streichinstrumente

F Stehen zwei Akkoladen auf einer Seite, werden sie durch zwei **Schrägstriche** voneinander abgetrennt.

G Steht hinter dem Instrumentennamen z.B. „in B" oder (B), handelt es sich um ein **transponierendes Instrument**. In diesem Fall deutet das (B) an, dass das notierte C als B erklingt, also alle Noten einen Ton tiefer erklingen als sie notiert sind. Die meisten transponierenden Instrumente sind in der Partitur durch diese Zusätze leicht zu erkennen. Es gibt aber auch transponierende Instrumente ohne eine entsprechende Angabe in der Partitur, wie z.B.:
Piccoloflöte (in c/eine Oktave höher)
Englischhorn (in f/eine Quinte tiefer)
Kontrafagott (in c/eine Oktave tiefer)
Kontrabass (in c/eine Oktave tiefer)

H Die transponierenden Blechblasinstrumente haben keine Generalvorzeichen, sondern bei Bedarf Versetzungszeichen, die direkt vor der jeweiligen Note stehen.

I Die Viola oder Bratsche wird im **Alt- bzw. Bratschenschlüssel** notiert, die Stimmen des Violoncellos und Fagotts manchmal im **Tenorschlüssel**. Beide Schlüssel sind leicht zu lesen, wenn man sich klarmacht, dass der Schlüssel den Ton c1 umrahmt, also:

Alt- Tenor- Violinschlüssel

= =

J Vor einem Wechsel der Ton- oder Taktart steht immer ein **Doppelstrich**. Das hier folgende Alla-Breve-Zeichen (¢) ist ebenso wie das Zeichen für den 4/4-Takt (c) ein Relikt aus einer älteren Notationspraxis und steht für den 2/2-Takt.

B
A
C
D
E
F
G
H
I
J
4
29
34
Fl.
Ob.
Cl. (B♭)
Fag.
Cor. (B♭)
Tr. (B♭)
Timp.
Vl.
I
II
Vla.
Vc.
Cb.
sfp
dim.
pp
arco
ff
cresc.

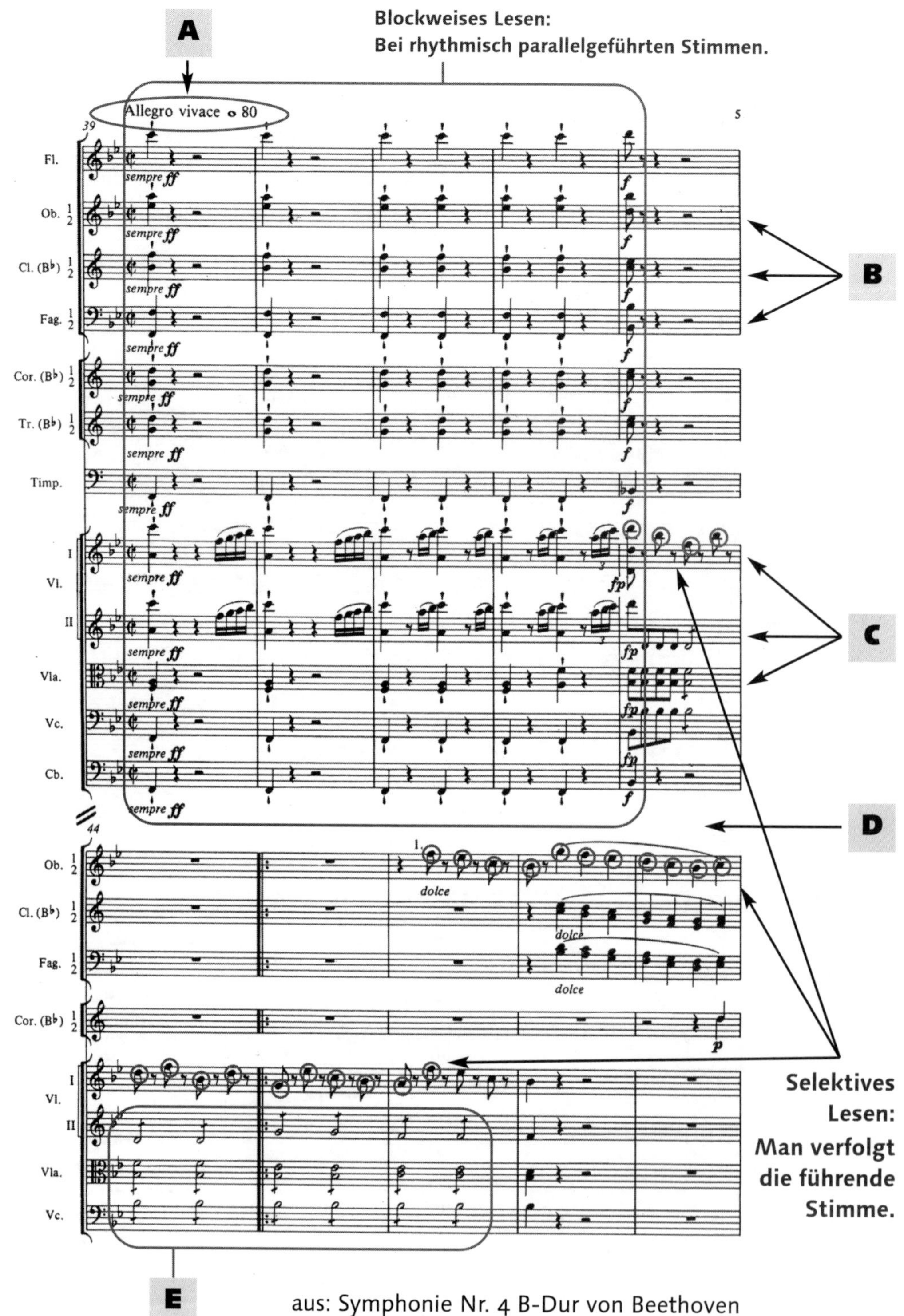

aus: Symphonie Nr. 4 B-Dur von Beethoven

A Durch die **Tempoangabe** (manchmal mit einer Metronomzahl verbunden) gibt der Komponist an, wie schnell ein Stück gespielt werden soll.

B Bei den Bläsern werden in der Regel zwei Stimmen in einer Notenzeile zusammengefasst. Spielen sie den gleichen Ton, erhält der Notenkopf zwei Hälse oder es steht a2 darüber.

C Zweistimmige Akkorde in den Notensystemen der Streicher werden von einem Spieler gespielt. Will man die Stimmen aufteilen, schreibt man **divisi** (geteilt). Dann spielt an jedem Pult ein Spieler die oberen und ein Spieler die unteren Noten.

D Hat eine Stimme, wie hier die Flöte, längere Zeit Pause, wird ihr Notensystem oft bis zum erneuten Einsatz der Stimme weggelassen. So wird Platz gespart, man muß weniger blättern und die erklingenden Stimmen sind übersichtlicher angeordnet.

E Um Platz zu sparen und Tonfolgen übersichtlicher zu gestalten, verwendet man gelegentlich sogenannte **Abbreviaturen (Faulenzer)**. Das hier verwendete Zeichen 𝅗𝅥 steht für ♩♩♩♩, wobei die Halbe Note die Dauer der Wiederholungen anzeigt und der Strich durch den Notenhals den Wert der zu wiederholenden Noten (1 Strich = Achtel, 2 = Sechzehntel usw.). Vgl. auch die Viola in T. 43, in der zunächst die Repetitionen ausgeschrieben und dann abgekürzt sind.

Partiturlesen im Klassensatz

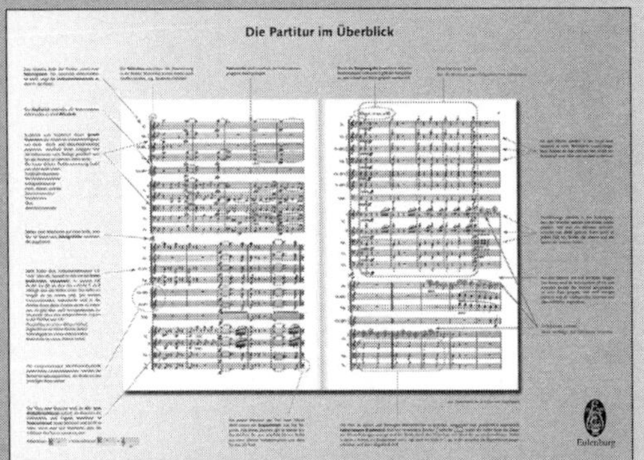

Diese kurze Einführung können Sie als kostenloses Faltblatt bestellen – gern auch im Klassensatz!

Faltblatt "Die Kunst des Partiturlesens"
Bestellnummer: ETP 9999-99 (kostenlos)

Die passende Ergänzung für Klassen- und Unterrichtsräume:

Plakat A2 "Die Partitur im Überblick"
Bestellnummer ETP 9950-99 (kostenlos)

Mozart im Klassensatz

Ein Lebens- und Reisebild

Mozart war nicht nur einer der größten Komponisten, sondern auch einer der besten Pianisten des 18. Jahrhunderts. Wie heutige Virtousen verbrachte er große Teile seines Lebens auf Konzertreisen zwischen den führenden Höfen und großen Städten seiner Zeit. Diese kleine Broschüre entfaltet ein Panorama des europäischen Musiklebens, das den Hintergrund für Mozarts Schaffen bildete. Eine Kurzbiographie und ein kleiner Einblick in seine Schreibweise runden das Bild ab.

Faltblatt "Mozart. Ein Lebens- und Reisebild"
Bestellnummer ETP 9990-99 (kostenlos)

Weitere Informationen unter www.eulenburg.de

Eulenburg

1507_01_MA 06/06